MAY − 5 2016

3 1994 01545 7341

SANTA ANA PUBLIC LIBRARY

D1121444

BOMBS, MINES, AND IEDS

J 623.45 WOO
Wood, Alix
Bombs, mines, and IEDs

$26.25
NEW HOPE   31994015457341

ALIX WOOD

PowerKiDS press™

NEW YORK

Published in 2016 by **Rosen Publishing**
29 East 21st Street, New York, NY 10010

Cataloging-in-Publication Data
Wood, Alix.
Bombs, mines, and IEDs / by Alix Wood.
p. cm. — (Today's high-tech weapons)
Includes index.
ISBN 978-1-5081-4675-9 (pbk.)
ISBN 978-1-5081-4676-6 (6-pack)
ISBN 978-1-5081-4677-3 (library binding)
1. Explosives — Juvenile literature. 2. Land mines — Juvenile literature.
3. Improvised explosive devices. I. Wood, Alix. II. Title.
TP270.5 W66 2016
662'.2—d23

Copyright © 2016 Alix Wood Books

All rights reserved. No part of this book may be reproduced in any form
without permission in writing from the publisher, except by a reviewer.

Editor: Eloise Macgregor
Designer: Alix Wood
Consultant: Mark Baker

Photo Credits: Cover © Shutterstock/Eky Studio (top), © Shutterstock/
optimarc (ctr), © Shutterstock/Studio 37 (btm); 4, 5, 7, 9, 21 top, 24, 27
© DoD; 6, 11, 13 bottom, 26 top, 29 bottom © Dollar Photo Club; 8 ©
DoD/Sgt. Ethan E. Rocke; 10 © DoD/Lance Cpl. JonDior Ferrell; 12 ©
DoD/Sgt. Margaret Taylor; 13 top © DoD/Master Sgt. Adrian Cadiz; 14
© DoD/Senior Airman Steven R. Doty; 15 © MoD; 16, 20 © U.S. Air
Force; 17 © DoD/Staff Sgt. Michael B. Keller; 18 © Dod/Capt. Patrick
Nichols; 19 © Fl295; 21 bottom © MoD/Sgt. Barry Pope; 22 © DoD/
Armen Shamlian; 23 © DoD/Charles Levy; 25 © DoD/Gertrud Zach;
26 bottom © DoD/Sgt. Mike MacLeod; 27 top © Gooutside; 28 © DoD/
Mass Communications; 29 top © DoD/Lt. Cmdr. John L. Kline

Manufactured in the United States of America
CPSIA Compliance Information: Batch #BW16PK.
For Further Information contact Rosen Publishing, New York, New York at 1-800-237-9932

CONTENTS

D.I.Y. BOMBS

Walking along a path through the Vietnam jungle, the first soldier in the line spots something. He quickly raises his hand to tell his team to stop. On the ground in front of him is an old tin can. It seems innocent enough, but it looks out of place. That soldier has just saved his whole team. The tin contained an IED.

IED is short for "improvised explosive device." These homemade bombs are often made out of captured military explosives. Thirty-three percent of U.S. casualties during the Vietnam War were caused by hidden IEDs and mines.

The "Grenade in a Can" was a booby trap used during the Vietnam War. A hand grenade was put in a tin can, with the safety pin removed. The can held the safety lever shut, which kept the grenade from exploding. If anyone kicked the can, or set off the trip wire, the grenade would fly out of the can and explode.

This deadly IED captured during the war in Iraq is made up of four artillery shells and an antitank mine wired together.

IEDs come in many different shapes and sizes. They can be triggered by **remote control**. They can also be triggered by the victim walking through an **infrared** or magnetic trigger, or stepping on pressure-sensitive bars or trip wires. IEDs usually have a switch to activate them, an explosive, a fuse to set off the explosive, a container, and a power source. Some may contain objects such as nails to injure more people.

IED FACT FILE:

NAME: IED stands for Improvised Explosive Device

APPEARANCE: IEDs can be all shapes and sizes

USES: They can be used to destroy vehicles or people. They can also be used to distract the enemy while preparing for an attack.

EFFECTIVENESS: Devices vary, but IEDs usually contain explosives often with nails, rocks, or other harmful objects

DEFENSE AGAINST IEDS: Finding them and disposing of them

COMBATING IEDs

A U.S. Marine spotter on patrol near Habbaniyah, Iraq, noticed a man videotaping some military vehicles. A high-powered rifle lay on the seat next to the man. When soldiers searched his car, they discovered explosives and IED-making materials. The attack was stopped in its tracks. Soldiers are trained to be suspicious of unusual behavior, or any unattended packages. IEDs are often placed along roads, fences, buildings, or even in trash piles.

The U.S. military wear blast-proof armor known as Tactical Vests. The bulletproof fabric gives some protection against blasts and bullets. Ceramic plates placed inside the vests also protect against threats such as armor-piercing rifle rounds.

U.S. Marines practice wearing their Modular Tactical Vests.

A Mine Resistant Ambush Protected (MRAP) vehicle has a V-shaped underside. This moves the force of an explosion around the vehicle rather than into it.

The best way to protect against IEDs is to understand and to watch the enemy. The military train to:
- **observe** the enemy, watch any suspicious activity in the area, and any movement of supplies and money
- **detect** the IEDs themselves
- **protect** people from a detected IED
- **dispose** of the detected IED
- **train** soldiers to be alert

The military can find, disrupt, and disable IEDs using new technology. Radio frequency **jamming** devices can disrupt cell phone signals often used to trigger IEDs. High-frequency radio pulses can destroy nearby IED electronics. Microwave-pulsing devices can "fry" the electronics of IEDs, and **lasers** can detect IED explosives within 100 feet (30 m). The military is starting to use robots and **drones** to help detect IEDs, carry out searches, and explode suspicious packages.

SUICIDE BOMBERS

One day in 2005, soldiers from the 3rd Infantry Division's Combat Team stopped a suspicious car at a checkpoint just north of Baghdad, Iraq. The vehicle was being prepared to be a deadly car bomb. Although there were no explosives yet, the car was wired with a **detonator**. Later, soldiers fired at a second vehicle as it tried to run through the checkpoint. The driver was killed, but two armed men tried to flee. One man was wounded. When the soldiers approached the wounded man, they saw he was wearing a **suicide belt** containing plastic explosives.

A vehicle is searched for weapons at a military checkpoint in Iraq.

Some **extremists** have been known to wear bombs strapped to themselves in order to get close to a target. A suicide belt or suicide vest is a belt or vest packed with explosives and armed with a detonator. The belts are usually filled with objects such as ball bearings, to cause the most casualties in the explosion. Obviously the person wearing the belt or vest will also die.

The military are trained to spot anyone wearing unusually bulky clothing. Infrared detectors can also be used to find explosives. A suspected suicide bomber is made to stand away from other people, and to remove any upper clothing until they can be disarmed.

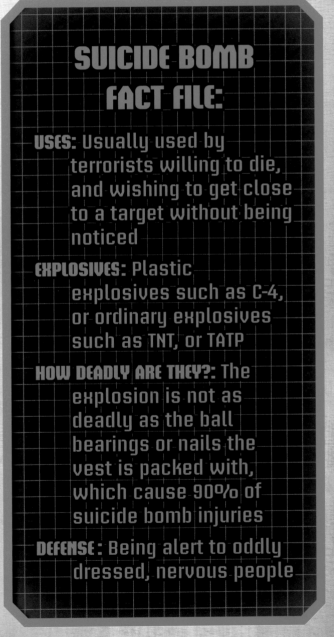

SUICIDE BOMB FACT FILE:

USES: Usually used by terrorists willing to die, and wishing to get close to a target without being noticed

EXPLOSIVES: Plastic explosives such as C-4, or ordinary explosives such as TNT, or TATP

HOW DEADLY ARE THEY?: The explosion is not as deadly as the ball bearings or nails the vest is packed with, which cause 90% of suicide bomb injuries

DEFENSE: Being alert to oddly dressed, nervous people

DETECTION DOGS

In 1972, Trans World Airlines' headquarters received a bomb threat. The airline began grounding all of its flights. TWA Flight 7, from New York to Los Angeles, was in the air when the pilot got the message. He turned back to New York and rushed everyone off the plane.

A trained German Shepherd detection dog named Brandy sniffed a black briefcase marked "crew," and sat down next to it. Inside, police found enough C-4 explosive to destroy the plane! Bomb-sniffing dogs were not used at that time. Brandy was in JFK airport by chance, taking part in a demonstration showing how dogs may possibly be used in the future to find bombs!

Military dog trainers teach trainee sniffer dogs to be interested in the smell of explosives. If the dog sniffs explosives, it gets a reward. After many repeats, the dog then learns to seek the smell. If an explosive is hidden, and the dog follows the scent, it's rewarded again.

A working dog examines a truck in Afghanistan.

A sniffer dog at work

A fully trained military detection dog runs ahead of troops, sniffing the area and searching for bombs, mines, and IEDs. If it smells explosives, it sits. When the dog sits, the troops stop. The dog runs back to its handler for its treat, and the bomb disposal team gets to work.

Dogs have a very strong sense of smell. Their noses are longer and larger than ours, so they can breathe in more air each time they sniff. Dogs also have 20 to 40 times more **odor receptors** in their noses than we do.

AIMING BOMBS AT THEIR TARGET

Bombers are aircraft designed to carry and drop bombs on enemy targets. To make sure the bombs are dropped in the correct place, high-tech equipment is used to guide the bomb to its target.

Laser-guided weapons use on-board electronics to track targets. The target is lit by a laser to identify it. Ground forces usually light the target for the missile to hone in on. In some cases, the attacking aircraft or a support aircraft may light the target instead. Laser-guided bombs are much more accurate than unguided bombs, and are used by the military worldwide.

The specialized ground forces, known as the Tactical Air Control Party, are responsible for guiding the weapons to their target using laser light beams (left). The beam can only be seen using night vision, so the TACPs can light up a target without the enemy knowing.

Early bombers used devices known as **bombsights** to help figure out the path a bomb would take once released from the aircraft. Bombsights helped figure out how the forces of gravity and air drag would affect the bomb.

Modern aircraft use computerized systems to manage their bombs, guns, missiles, and navigation. The system can work out how a bomb will fall. It can adjust for weather, **altitude**, moving targets, and the climb and dive angle of the aircraft! The information can be displayed on the cockpit window, known as a "head-up display."

HUD FACT FILE:

WHAT IS HUD?: HUD stands for Head-Up Display

HOW DOES IT WORK?: Information is displayed on the cockpit windshield, so the pilot does not have to look down at the aircraft's instruments

WHAT DOES IT DISPLAY?: The display shows the target, speed of approach, range, direction, and the weapons available

Head-Up Display

instruments

SMART BOMBS

The U.S. Air Force laser-guided bombing during the 1990s Gulf War was accurate in clear conditions. If dust, smoke, fog, or cloud covered the area, the electronics couldn't find the target. Research began to find a solution.

GPS (global positioning system) was fairly new at the time. Boeing used GPS to develop a system known as JDAM (Joint Direct Attack **Munition**). JDAM turns an ordinary "dumb" bomb into a "smart" bomb. The kit includes an adjustable tail fin, a control computer, a guidance system, and a GPS receiver.

A "dumb" bomb equipped with JDAM equipment

adjustable tail fins

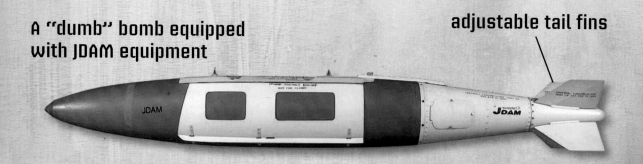

Just before releasing the bomb, the aircraft's computer gives the bomb's computer its current position and the GPS position of the target. In the air, the GPS receiver uses signals from GPS satellites to update its position. The control system adjusts the fins to "steer" the bomb in the right direction.

According to the U.S. Air Force, the system is accurate to within 40 feet (13 m). The bombs generally hit within a few feet of their target. Weapons Effectiveness Teams often follow up bombing raids by taking tape measures and checking the accuracy of each hit. A JDAM bomb can take out a single building and leave the rest of the neighborhood standing!

F-15E Strike Eagles dropping 2,000-pound JDAMs on a cave in Afghanistan.

JDAM FACT FILE:

WHAT BOMBS CAN JDAM BE ATTACHED TO?: At present JDAMs have been used on 500-, 1,000-, and 2,000-pound bombs

HOW ACCURATE ARE THEY?: JDAM bombs are very accurate. JDAM has been listed in the Guinness Book of Records as the world's most accurate bomb.

FUTURE DEVELOPMENTS: The Australian military is working on a new design with wings that unfold, which will possibly triple the range the bombs can travel

DAISY CUTTERS, MOABs, AND FOABs

The BLU-82 is a massive 15,000-pound (6,800 kg) bomb. It was designed to create an instant clearing in the jungles of Vietnam. It was nicknamed "daisy cutter" as it could flatten a forest into a helicopter landing zone in minutes! The bomb was used in Afghanistan to **intimidate** the enemy because of its very large blast. It is one of the largest conventional weapons ever to be used.

BLU-82 FACT FILE:

WHAT DOES BLU MEAN?: BLU stands for Bomb Live Unit. Bomb Dummy Units (BDUs) are bombs used for practice.

IS IT DANGEROUS TO DROP? Due to its powerful blast, the bomber must be at a height of 6,000 feet (1,800 m) above ground level before releasing this weapon

The enormous blast from a BLU-82 as it explodes over a military testing range in Utah

The Massive Ordnance Air Blast (MOAB), commonly known as the Mother of All Bombs, is a 30-foot (9.1 m) bomb. The bomb is so large it has to be pushed out the back of a cargo plane on a pallet! The MOAB is then guided by satellite to its target. It bursts around 6 feet (1.8 m) above the ground. A bomb that hits the ground and bursts sends much of its energy into the ground or into the air. An air-burst weapon is more effective because it sends most of its energy out to the side.

The MOAB used to be the largest nonnuclear bomb in the world. Russia has since developed the "Father of All Bombs". Thought to be four times as powerful as the MOAB, the FOAB is designed to explode in midair and deliver a huge shock wave to the target area below.

MOAB FACT FILE:

TYPE: Conventional, nonnuclear bomb

WEIGHT: The bomb weighs 21,000 lbs (9,525 kg)

EXPLOSIVES: 18,000 pounds of tritonal. Tritonal is a mixture of TNT (80%) and aluminum powder (20%).

CONTROL: A GPS receiver moves the tail fins to change the direction of the bomb as it falls

BOMB SQUADS

They call it the "Long Walk." There can't be many things more terrifying than walking toward an unexploded bomb. This is the job of the bomb disposal teams, known as Explosive Ordnance Technicians. Enemy bombs, mines, and IEDs must be disarmed. Your own side's shells, bombs, and munitions may also have failed to explode, leaving them scattered dangerously around the battlefield. You put on your protective suit and start your lonely walk toward the danger.

A blast suit is a heavy suit of body armor made to help withstand the blast of a bomb and protect the wearer. Bomb suits don't have any hand protection, as the technician needs bare hands to work with. The suit is usually made from a strong material known as Kevlar, foam, and plastic.

A robot investigating a suspected IED

Technicians use special robots to disarm bombs. Using a video transmitter and a controller, the operator can see the bomb and guide the robot. Different grippers can be attached. The robot can even do an **x-ray** to see inside suspicious packages! Steel tracks allow the robot to climb steep slopes.

If a bomb is in a busy area, technicians will try to move it to a different location. If that's not possible, they use sand bags, tunnels, and ditches to try to cut down on any possible damage to the area. If a bomb is in an open area, such as the one below, a technician will safely blow it up using explosives.

HIROSHIMA

At around 2:00 a.m. on August 6, 1945, the U.S. B-29 Superfortress bomber, *Enola Gay*, left the island of Tinian. It was heading for Hiroshima, Japan. At 6:00 a.m., the pilot, Colonel Paul Tibbets, told his crew they were carrying an atomic bomb. By 8:09 a.m., Hiroshima had disappeared under a cloud of smoke and fire.

During World War II, scientists had discovered that a powerful explosion was possible by splitting an atom. Although by 1945 the U.S. war with Japan was almost over, Japan had not surrendered. Invading Japan would cost many U.S. lives. President Truman decided to drop the atomic bomb instead.

The explosion over Hiroshima was devastating. The city was destroyed. Tens of thousands of people were killed. When copilot Captain Robert Lewis looked down at the destruction they had left behind, he is reported to have said "My God, what have we done?"

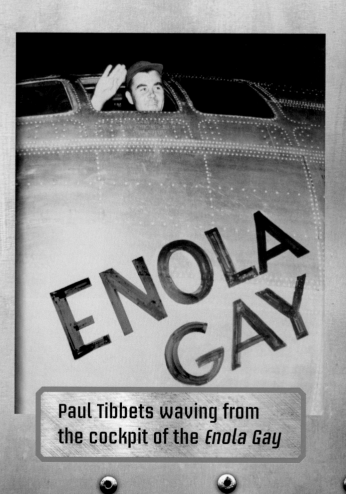

Paul Tibbets waving from the cockpit of the *Enola Gay*

The atom bombs exploding over Hiroshima (left) and Nagasaki (right)

Despite the bombing, Japan still refused to surrender. Three days later another atomic bomb was dropped on Nagasaki, Japan. Six days after the bombing of Nagasaki, Japan surrendered. The two bombings killed at least 129,000 people. They are, to date, the only time nuclear weapons have been used for warfare in history.

ATOM BOMB FACT FILE:

TYPE: Nuclear bomb

CODE NAMES: Hiroshima's bomb code name was "Little Boy" and Nagasaki's was named "Fat Man"

HOW DEADLY?: Atomic bombs cause a deadly blast and fireball. After the blast, **radiation** and **radioactive** rain can cause cancer and contaminate areas for many years.

HIDDEN DANGER

In a field in Kurdistan some children head out to play. Unknown to them, hidden under leaves and rocks is an antipersonnel blast mine. Land mines are triggered to explode by pressure, a tripwire, or remote detonation.

During the war between Iran and Iraq, landmines were placed on the outskirts of cities and villages. Because they were not cleared quickly at the end of the conflict, wind, rain, and landslides have caused them to move. Now, the job of finding and clearing them is even harder than it would have been.

A Russian antitank mine

Landmines are used during wars as "area denial" weapons. That means they make an area unsafe for anyone to enter. Area denial weapons cannot tell if a person is a friend or an enemy. New area denial weapons which can sense if someone is the enemy are being researched, but are not yet ready to use.

U.S. Army soldiers set up a mine during training.

There are "smart" and "dumb" mines. Smart mines self-destruct automatically after a period of time. Dumb mines last indefinitely, and remain dangerous after a war is over. Smart mines might be used by U.S. forces to slow down advancing enemy forces, but they make sure no active mines are left behind afterward.

LANDMINE FACT FILE:

TYPES: Antipersonnel mines are designed to injure people. Antitank mines have more explosive and are designed to disable tanks and other vehicles.

HOW DO SMART MINES WORK?: Smart mines are designed to self-destruct if they are not set off within a span of four hours to 15 days. If the self-destruct mechanism fails to work, the battery will go dead within 90 days.

HOW LONG DO DUMB MINES LAST?: Dumb mines can stay active for more than 50 years after they were put in the ground

FINDING MINES

The military has developed many ways to find mines and make them safe. Most **minesweeping** is done using metal detectors or vehicles fitted with specialist tools. Some modern mines are made using little metal, so that metal detectors can't find them.

Ground Penetrating Radar (GPR) can find nonmetallic mines. It is also set off by objects such as tree roots and stones and even changes in soil moisture, though. A combined GPR and standard metal detector is being developed for the future.

metal detector

A soldier throws a grappling hook to clear a safe path. The hook will set off any mines up ahead.

Mine clearers sometimes use rats to sniff out explosives! Because they don't weigh much, the rat won't set off the mine. The trained rat wears a harness connected to a rope, stretched between two handlers. They sweep up and down an area and the rat is trained to scratch the ground if it smells a mine!

Special vehicles, such as the mine-clearing vehicle pictured below, can be driven through the minefield, deliberately detonating the mines it drives over. The vehicles are designed to withstand the explosions. Some are operated by a driver, and some are operated using remote control.

MINES UNDER THE SEA

A naval mine is an explosive device placed in the water. They are designed to damage or destroy ships and submarines. Mines have become very high-tech. They can be disguised to look like seaweed or rocks. Some rest on the ocean floor, while some float, or are anchored at different heights under the surface of the water. Some mines have sensors that can tell if a passing ship fits their intended target's size, shape, or speed!

Mines blow up when struck by a target, or triggered by remote control. Some mines explode if they sense changes in the magnetic field. Because of this, U.S. Navy minesweepers' hulls are made of wood or glass fiber, not metal. Everything on board is nonmagnetic. They don't even allow metal coat hangers!

A U.S. Navy minesweeper ship detonates an underwater mine during a training exercise.

The navy uses special equipment to safely set off the explosives. Floating mines are destroyed by cutting their mooring wire. Mines can be detonated by dragging a dummy ship, known as a "sled," which sets off the mine. Mines can also be hunted using sonar. Once found, they can then be destroyed by divers or by remote-controlled unmanned mini submarines.

A U.S. Navy Sea Dragon towing a minesweeping sled

NAVAL MINES FACT FILE:

LAYING MINES: Naval mines can be laid easily by ship, from aircraft, or even from a truck parked on a bridge

HOW DEADLY?: Damage depends on how close a ship is to the blast and how much explosive is used. A mine can easily sink a large ship.

Dolphins have been trained to hunt and mark mines by the U.S. Navy. Dolphins were used in the Persian Gulf during the Iraq War and helped clear more than 100 mines and booby traps.

GLOSSARY

altitude: The height above Earth's surface.

bombsights: A mechanical or electronic device used in an aircraft for aiming bombs.

conventional weapons: Weapons in wide use; not weapons of mass destruction such as nuclear, biological, and chemical weapons.

detonator: A device used to set of another explosive.

drones: An aircraft or ship without a pilot that is controlled by radio signals.

extremists: People who believe in and support extreme ideas, especially in politics.

infrared: Light waves that are outside of the visible part of the light range at the red end, which we can see.

intimidate: To make shy or afraid by threats.

jamming: To make impossible to understand by sending out interfering signals or messages.

lasers: Devices that use vibrations of atoms or molecules to generate a narrow beam of light.

minesweeping: The act of removing or destroying mines.

munition: A military weapon, ammunition, or equipment.

nuclear: Having to do with the power created by splitting atoms.

odor receptors: Special cells in the nose that sense smell.

proboscis: An insect's elongated sucking mouthpart.

radiation: Rays of light, heat, or energy that spread outward from something.

radioactive: Giving off rays of light, heat, or energy.

remote control: To control a device by means of radio or infrared signals.

suicide belt: A belt packed with explosives and armed with a detonator.

terrorists: People or groups that scare or threaten with violence illegally.

x-ray: Rays that can pass through matter that light rays cannot.

FOR MORE INFORMATION

BOOKS

Baxter, Roberta. *The Dropping of the Atomic Bombs: A History Perspectives Book*. North Mankato, MN: Cherry Lake Publishing, 2014.

Bearce, Stephanie. *Top Secret Files: The Cold War: Secrets, Special Missions, and Hidden Facts about the CIA, KGB, and MI6*. Austin, TX: Prufrock Press, 2015.

Ross, Stewart. *Hiroshima* (Place in History). London, UK: Arcturus Publishing, 2011.

Zullo, Allan. *10 True Tales: War Heroes From Iraq*. New York, NY: Scholastic Nonfiction, 2014.

Due to the changing nature of Internet links, PowerKids Press has developed an online list of websites related to the subject of this book. This site is updated regularly. Please use this link to access the list:
www.powerkidslinks.com/thtw/bombs

INDEX